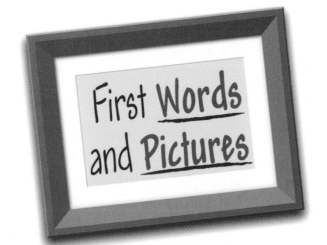

First Words and **Pictures**

A World of Colours

By Ruth Owen, Emma Randall and Sophie Murphy

Published in 2017 by Ruby Tuesday Books Ltd.

Copyright © 2017 Ruby Tuesday Books Ltd.

Editor: Mark J. Sachner
Production: John Lingham

Photo Credits:
Photographs courtesy of Shutterstock

British Library Cataloguing In Publication Data (CIP)
is available for this title.

ISBN 978-1-911341-66-6

Printed in Poland by L&C Printing Group

What's Inside the Book?

There are colours all around us!

teddy bear

tricycle

duck

Can you say the colours of the toys?

bricks

panda

Plasticine

flowers

monkey

rackets

balls

Let's discover colours!

cat
white

dog
black

Black and White

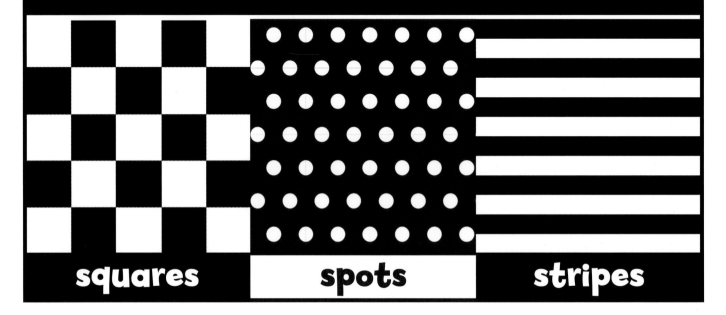

squares

spots

stripes

football

cow

black and white

snow

keyboard

milk

car

fire engine

Let's Discover Red

trainers

boots

8

knife

fork

spoon

house

heart

plate

shoes

poppy

bowl

butterfly

blue sky

What colour
are the clouds?

Let's Discover Blue

bluebells

blue eyes

blueberries

cup

scissors

What colours are the scissors?

saucer

van

lorry

yellow

digger

dump truck

Let's Discover Yellow

raincoat

hat

sunflower

grater

cheese

lemon

star

frying pan

eggs

pasta

yolk

13

chalk

How Do We Make Art?

pencils

crayons

face paints

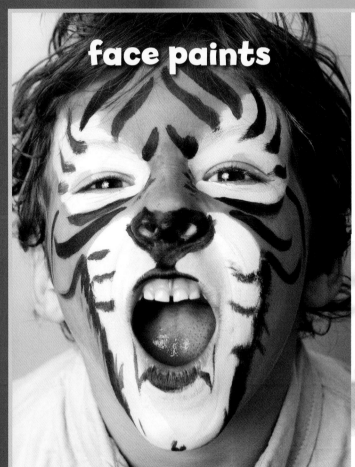

paintbrushes

paint

marker pens

We can mix colours to make new colours.

When we mix blue and yellow we make green!

Let's Discover Green

grasshopper

guinea pig

grass

jumper

umbrella

leaf

trowel

dustpan

brush

garden
fork

dinosaur

17

When we mix red and yellow we make orange!

Let's Discover Orange

autumn leaf

tree

fire

bucket

scarf

pumpkin big

ice lolly

little

What colours can you see on the tiger?

T-shirt

tiger

19

When we mix red and blue we make purple!

Let's Discover Purple

glasses

buttons

gloves

dress

ice cream

skirt

toothbrush

watch

beetle

When we mix red and white we make pink!

Let's Discover Pink

pyjamas

tongue

shirt

flip flops

cake

balloons

What colours are the stripey socks?

sock

straw

clock

milkshake

When we mix blue and orange we make brown!

Let's Discover Brown

pine cone

mud

bird

chocolate

bag

rucksack

trousers

acorn

ukulele

biscuit

toucan

orange

beak

crab

Animal Colours

yellow

snake

ladybird

red

brown **puppy**

pink piglet

blue

fish

zebra

black
white

What colours do you
see on this frog?

peas

blackberries

satsuma

Fruit and Vegetables

strawberry

cucumber

banana

peel

slice

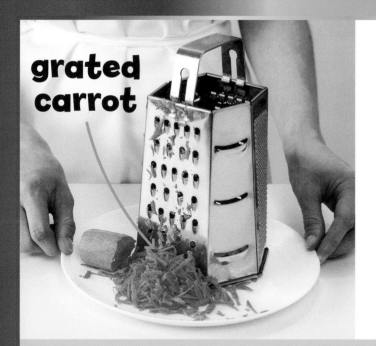

grated carrot

apple

slice

What colour is your favourite fruit or vegetable?

tomato

half

corn on the cob

Tips and Ideas

Look ✓ Read ✓ Talk ✓ Discover ✓ Learn ✓

This book is designed to help you and your child get the best learning experience possible. We suggest that you make yourselves comfortable within a quiet environment and allow your child to hold the book and turn the pages. When you and your child are reading the book, pause to allow your child to *read* a word or ask questions about the pictures and words.

Pages 4-5: Point each toy out individually and encourage your child to say and read what it is.

Page 7: If you do not have snow, ask your child to describe the colour and texture of ice cubes. Allow the snow or ice cubes to melt and discuss the changes in colour from white to clear.

Pages 8-9: Point to the photographs on the pages and allow the child to read the text and explore the different words they see. What is the child doing with the welly boots?

Page 10: Encourage your child to repeat words that are often used between the two of you. Go outside and look at the moving clouds. Notice and discuss the change in the colours of the clouds from a bright day to a rainy day.

Page 12: Try blending sounds for your child to hear and then repeat. For example, the girl is wearing a H-A-T (hat).

Page 15: Encourage your child to mix and explore paint colours using paintbrushes, sponges or even their hands!

Page 17: Collect differently coloured leaves and ask your child to discuss the leaves' different colours, textures and shapes.

Page 19: When your child next has an ice lolly, encourage him or her to choose a colour. Ask your child to touch the lolly and explain how it feels on their hands.

Page 20: Ask your child if he or she can spot any purple objects around you.

Page 22: Mix red and white paint together. Add different materials to create textures for your child to touch and discuss. For example, try adding sand, glitter, shredded paper or sawdust.

Page 24: Mix blue and orange paint together with your child to make brown. Talk through the gradual colour change process. Add black paint to darken the brown, or add white to lighten the brown.

Page 26: Ask your child to point to or say the different colours on an animal. For example, if you have a pet this might include fur, eyes, nose or tongue. Go outside and look at birds or insects, or visit a farm, zoo or aquarium and discuss the differently coloured animals.

Page 28: Allow your child to watch you prepare food and discuss with him or her the noticeable changes that happen – for example, chopping, slicing, grating and blending. Discuss any colour changes that happen when foods are mixed.

Colour Activities

Let's Make Colours!

In a tough tray (or other shallow, washable container) place a selection of differently coloured paints and tools, such as paintbrushes, sponges, rollers or spoons.

Encourage your child to mix the paints together while you ask open questions.

• What colour paints can you see in the tray?

• What other objects can you see around us that are the same colours?

• What will happen if we add white paint? Show me.

You can add materials to the paint to allow your child to feel and discuss different textures – for example, sawdust, glitter or crushed chalk.

• What does the paint feel like with glitter in it? (Or another material.)

Mixing Colours with Ice

Pour water into an ice cube tray. Add different food colours to the sections in the tray and place into the freezer. Once the water has frozen, place the ice cubes onto a water-resistant mat or tray.

Ask your child to spot the different colours within the ice. Watch as the ice cubes begin to melt and explain how the colours are mixing together and creating new colours.

Go On a Colourful Nature Treasure Hunt

Go on a walk with your child in a garden, park or woodland. Encourage your child to collect natural objects – for example, leaves, grass, sticks, flowers and pebbles.

Once your child has collected lots of objects, encourage him or her to sort the objects into groups of matching colours. Discuss with your child the different colour shades of the objects within each group.